Navigating SAM.gov

The Small Business Owner's Complete Registration Guide

From Registration to Ready to Win:

Everything You Need to Register Your Business,

Get Certified, and Compete for Federal Contracts

Pen 2 Paper Publishers

pen2paperpublishers.com

For permission requests, contact the publisher at:

Pen 2 Paper Publishers

hello@pen2paperpublishers.com

pen2paperpublishers.com

First Edition, 2026

ISBN 979-8-9958776-0-8 (Paperback)

ISBN 979-8-9958776-1-5 (eBook)

Disclaimer

This guide is intended for informational and educational purposes only. The information contained herein reflects SAM.gov processes, federal regulations, and agency contact information as verified at the time of publication. Government systems, processes, and contact information are subject to change.

This publication does not constitute legal, financial, or professional advice. The author and publisher make no representations or warranties of any kind, express or implied, about the completeness, accuracy, reliability, or suitability of the information contained herein.

Readers are encouraged to verify current requirements directly with the relevant federal agencies before taking action. For legal or financial matters related to government contracting, consult a qualified attorney or financial advisor.

Pen 2 Paper Publishers is not affiliated with, endorsed by, or sponsored by SAM.gov, the U.S. General Services Administration, the U.S. Small Business Administration, or any other federal agency.

This guide is dedicated to every small business owner who looked at the federal contracting system and thought,

"I don't know where to start."

With this guide, you can take your first step with confidence.

How to Use This Guide

This guide meets you wherever you are in the federal contracting process. Make the most of it by following these tips:

If you are brand new to SAM.gov:

Read from beginning to end. Each chapter builds on the one before it. Start with Chapter 2 to gather your documents, move through Chapters 3 and 4 to complete your registration, and continue through the guide in the order it appears.

If you are partway through registration:

Jump right to the chapter where you are stuck. Each chapter stands alone as a reference. Use the chapter list in Chapter 1 to find exactly what you need.

If you are already registered:

Focus on Chapters 7, 8, and 9 for certification, maintenance, and opportunity finding. Chapter 10 is your permanent reference section for contacts, resources, and the glossary.

If you hit an error or problem:

Go directly to Chapter 5. It covers the top 10 SAM.gov errors with verified fixes, along with the exact contact information for every agency that can help.

> **Use This Guide as a Working Document**
>
> Write in it. Highlight it. Mark pages. Add your UEI and CAGE code to the notes pages. The more you use this guide, the more valuable it becomes. It is not meant to sit on a shelf — it is meant to go with you into the federal marketplace.

About Pen 2 Paper Publishers

Pen 2 Paper Publishers is an independent imprint creating concise, actionable resources for small business owners, entrepreneurs, and professionals in government and business systems. Our mission is to simplify complex processes into practical steps, ensuring accessibility for all backgrounds and experience levels.

Our expert-written publications address real challenges small business owners face. We focus on providing clear, honest, and trustworthy guidance so every business owner can confidently navigate regulatory and contracting environments.

Pen 2 Paper Publishers provides government contracting guides, business manuals, and resources for certification and professional development to help small business owners compete and achieve long-term success.

Connect With Pen 2 Paper Publishers

pen2paperpublishers.com

hello@pen2paperpublishers.com

info@pen2paperpublishers.com

A note on accuracy:

This guide reflects SAM.gov processes and agency contact information as of the date of publication. As you progress, remember that government systems change. When in doubt, verify with the agency using contacts in Chapter 10 before moving forward.

CHAPTER ONE

Introduction: Why SAM.gov Matters and Why You Picked Up This Guide

Most small businesses never pursue federal contracts — not for lack of qualifications, but because no one has shown them how. The federal government spends over $600 billion every year on goods and services from businesses just like yours. That money exists. That opportunity is real. And now, you are ready to claim it.

The System That Opens the Door

SAM.gov is the System for Award Management. It is the federal registration system for businesses wanting to work with the government. If your business isn't registered, federal agencies legally can't pay you. This rule applies no matter how qualified you are.

Registration is a requirement. It is the baseline. Without it, you are invisible to contracting officers, grant managers, and procurement officials. These officials control the budgets for your services.

With registration, you belong at the table.

Who This Guide Is For

This guide is for small business owners entering the federal marketplace. If you are opening SAM.gov for the first time and think, "What am I even looking at?" this is for you.

This guide was written for the entrepreneur who built something real and knows their services have value for the government. Someone who is ready for their expertise to be recognized and is determined not to remain the best-kept secret in their industry.

This guide is also for the business owner who began the registration, encountered an error, and stopped because clear next steps were never explained.

Wherever you are—new to SAM.gov or struggling with registration—this guide will walk you through every step. It offers clarity, honesty, and plain language rarely found in government instructions.

A Special Note for Women Business Owners

If you are a woman who owns and operates your business, this guide has something extra for you. Chapter 7 covers WOSB and EDWOSB certification in depth—the federal designations that unlock set-aside contracts reserved for women-owned businesses. Over $30.9 billion in federal contracts are set aside for women-owned businesses every year. That chapter alone is worth the price of this guide.

Why SAM.gov Is Worth Your Time

Let us be honest about something. SAM.gov is not a simple system. The government built it for itself, and the user experience shows that. There will be times in this process when you feel frustrated, confused, or ready to quit.

Before you get to those moments, here is why it is worth pushing through:

The Federal Marketplace Is the Largest in the World

No private-sector client has a budget like the federal government. Agencies operate year-round. They pay on time through electronic funds transfer. Contracts can bring stable, predictable revenue. This can supplement or even replace your commercial client work.

Law Protects Small Businesses

The federal government must award at least 23% of all contract dollars to small businesses. Within that, there are specific goals for women-owned, veteran-owned, minority-owned, and HUBZone businesses. This is not charity — it is the law. Contracting officers are measured on whether they find and award contracts to businesses like yours.

Registration Opens More Than One Door

Your SAM.gov registration is not just for federal contracts. You'll need it for most federal grant applications and for state government contracting in many states. It is also needed for subcontracting with large prime contractors. One registration gives you access to many opportunities beyond a single federal contract.

The Barrier to Entry Is the Opportunity

Your willingness to do what others won't is your unbeatable edge. Push past the barriers. What feels difficult now becomes your advantage tomorrow.

SAM.gov Registration Is Free

There is no cost to register your business in SAM.gov. The registration process is managed by the federal government and is completely free. If anyone charges you to register, they are not the government. Be cautious of third-party services that offer to register your business for a fee — you can do everything in this guide yourself at no cost.

What This Guide Covers

This guide takes you through the entire SAM.gov process, from document prep to contract strategies. Each chapter covers:

Ch.	Title	What You Will Learn
2	Before You Begin	Every document and piece of information you need to gather before touching SAM.gov, including a printable pre-registration checklist.
3	Creating Your Login.gov Account	Step-by-step instructions for creating the secure federal account that gives you access to SAM.gov.
4	Step-by-Step Registration	A complete walkthrough of every section of the SAM.gov registration, with screen descriptions at every critical step.
5	Common Errors and How to Fix Them	The top 10 SAM.gov errors with verified causes, fixes, and the exact contact information for every agency that can help.
6	Understanding Your UEI Number	What your Unique Entity Identifier is, where to find it, how it compares to the CAGE code, and how to use it effectively.

Ch.	Title	What You Will Learn
7	WOSB and EDWOSB Certification	A deep dive into women-owned business certifications, eligibility requirements, the free certification process, and how to find set-aside contracts.
8	Maintaining and Renewing	How to keep your registration active, what to update and when, and an annual renewal timeline that ensures you never miss a deadline.
9	Finding Opportunities	How to search SAM.gov for contracts, understand set-aside types, create your capability statement, and build your first 90-day action plan.
10	Resources and Glossary	A complete reference section with verified contact information for every key agency, a 25-term glossary, and your next steps roadmap.

Your Seat at the Table Is Waiting

The federal government spends over a billion dollars every business day. It needs consultants, administrators, analysts, trainers, writers, managers, and all kinds of service providers. It needs women-owned businesses. It needs businesses with fresh perspectives and community ties. The personal accountability of a small business owner is valuable.

You built a business worth serving. Now take action—use this guide to stand out, win contracts, and be found by the right people.

Your registration starts on the next page — let's go!

CHAPTER TWO

Before You Begin: Everything You Need to Register on SAM.gov

Before claiming your seat at the federal contracting table, make sure you have everything ready. This preparation is where your confidence begins. If anything seems unfamiliar, know others have faced the same challenge—and support is available at every step. Now, let's get specific about what to prepare before logging in to SAM.gov.

One common mistake owners make is starting the registration process without the necessary documents. SAM.gov can time out unexpectedly. It often asks for information you may not anticipate. Without preparation, a process that should take hours can turn into days of frustration. This guide is designed to prevent that experience.

This chapter is your preparation headquarters. Read it completely before you touch SAM.gov. Gather everything listed here first. Then, when you log in, you'll move through the process with confidence.

Your Legal Business Information

SAM.gov registers your business as a legal entity. You'll need your official business details exactly as they appear on your government and legal documents. Even a small difference, like a period after "LLC" or a name variation, can cause rejection.

Legal Business Name

Your legal business name is as it appears on your state's registration documents. For example: if your state has "Main Street Consulting LLC," enter exactly that in SAM.gov. Do not write "Main Street Consulting, LLC" with a comma. Do not use "MS Consulting." Use the exact name from your state registration.

> **Pro Tip**
>
> Pull out your state business registration certificate right now and set it next to your computer. Use it as your reference for every name field in SAM.gov.

Business Structure

Know your business structure before you begin. SAM.gov will ask you to identify your legal organization. Common structures include:

- Sole Proprietorship.
- Limited Liability Company (LLC).
- Corporation (S-Corp or C-Corp).
- Partnership.
- Nonprofit Organization.

Physical Business Address

You'll need your official business address — the address on file with the IRS and your state. If you use a P.O. Box for mail, that is fine for correspondence, but SAM.gov requires a physical address as your primary business location. A home address is perfectly acceptable if that is where your business operates.

Your EIN — Employer Identification Number

Your EIN is your business's tax identification number, assigned by the IRS. Think of it as your business's social security number. You will need this to register on SAM.gov, and it must match exactly what the IRS has on file for your business.

> **Don't have an EIN yet?**
>
> You can apply for free at irs.gov. You'll receive your EIN immediately upon completing the online application. Do this before you proceed.

Important: SAM.gov will validate your EIN directly with the IRS. This means the name you enter must match exactly the name the IRS has on file. If there is a mismatch, your registration will fail validation. We will cover how to handle this error in Chapter 5.

Your UEI — Unique Entity Identifier

The Unique Entity Identifier, or UEI, replaced the old DUNS number in April 2022. If you registered on SAM.gov before that date, your UEI was automatically assigned. If you are registering for the first time, SAM.gov will assign your UEI when you create your entity record.

You do not need to obtain your UEI separately before registering. SAM.gov generates it during the registration process. However, if you already have a UEI from a previous registration, have it on hand.

What happened to my DUNS number?

The DUNS number (managed by Dun & Bradstreet) is no longer used for federal government contracting. SAM.gov fully transitioned to the UEI system in 2022. Your DUNS is no longer required for any federal contracting or grant applications.

Your NAICS Codes

NAICS stands for North American Industry Classification System. These are numerical codes that classify the type of business you operate. When you register on SAM.gov, you will select the NAICS codes that best describe your business activities.

Choosing the right NAICS codes is one of the most strategic decisions you will make in this process. Federal contract opportunities are categorized by NAICS codes, and contracting officers search for vendors that match those codes in their solicitations. The wrong codes mean you could be invisible to the very opportunities you're qualified for.

How to find your NAICS codes

- Visit census.gov/naics to search by keyword.
- Search terms related to your services (e.g., "consulting," "administrative support," "professional services").
- You can select multiple NAICS codes — choose all that apply to your business.
- Identify your PRIMARY code — the one that represents your main service.

Write your NAICS codes down before you begin registration. You will need them in the Core Data section of SAM.gov.

Your Banking Information

SAM.gov requires your banking information to set up an Electronic Funds Transfer (EFT). This is how the federal government pays you when you are awarded a contract. Without valid banking information, your registration cannot be completed. You will need:

- Your bank's ABA routing number (the 9-digit number on the bottom left of a check).
- Your business checking account number.
- The name on the bank account (must match your business name).

> **Pro Tip** Use a dedicated business checking account for EFT payments, not a personal account. If you only have a personal account right now, it will work — but opening a business account should be on your to-do list before your first contract award.

Points of Contact

SAM.gov will ask you to designate points of contact for your registration. These are the people you can reach regarding your entity record and any associated contracts. You will need to provide:

- Full legal name.
- Business title.
- Email address.
- Phone number.

For most small businesses, this will be you — the owner. Make sure the email address you use is one you check regularly, as SAM.gov sends important notifications, including your annual renewal reminders, to your points of contact.

Your Complete Pre-Registration Checklist

Use this checklist to confirm you have everything ready before logging in to SAM.gov. Do not skip this step. Come back to this page and check off each item.

✓	Document / Information	Notes
☐	**Legal business name**	Exactly as it appears on your state registration
☐	**Business structure**	LLC, Sole Prop, Corp, etc.
☐	**Physical business address**	No P.O. Boxes for primary address
☐	**EIN (9-digit number)**	Must match IRS records exactly
☐	**State business registration**	Certificate or filing confirmation
☐	**NAICS codes**	Primary + any additional codes
☐	**Bank routing number**	9-digit ABA number from your check
☐	**Business account number**	Checking account for EFT payments
☐	**Point of contact info**	Name, title, email, phone
☐	**Login.gov account**	Create at login.gov before starting

You Are Ready. Let's go.

If you've checked every item on that list, you are more prepared than the majority of business owners who attempt to register on SAM.gov. That preparation is your advantage. It is about walking into this process with confidence rather than frustration.

In the next chapter, we will set up your Login.gov account — the secure gateway you'll use to access SAM.gov. This is a quick but important step, and I'll walk you through every screen so nothing catches you off guard.

You've got this. Let's keep moving.

Chapter 2 Key Takeaways

- Gather all documents before logging into SAM.gov — do not start without them.
- Your legal business name must match your IRS and state records exactly.
- Obtain your EIN from the IRS before you begin if you don't have one.
- Choose NAICS codes strategically — they determine which contracts find you.
- SAM.gov requires a physical address and dedicated business banking information — have your routing number, account number, and account name ready.
- Use the Pre-Registration Checklist on the previous page before proceeding.

CHAPTER THREE

Creating Your Login.gov Account: Your Gateway to SAM.gov

Before you can set foot inside SAM.gov, you need a key. That key is your Login.gov account.

Login.gov is the federal government's official single sign-on platform. It was created to give citizens and business owners one secure, trusted account to access multiple government websites — including SAM.gov, USAJobs, and many other federal systems. Think of it as your federal digital identity.

The good news is that creating your Login.gov account is straightforward and only needs to be done once. Once your account is set up, you can use it to access SAM.gov every time you log in. This chapter will walk you through every step so you arrive at SAM.gov ready to register.

> **Do This Before Anything Else**
>
> You cannot access SAM.gov to register your business without a Login.gov account. Complete this chapter fully before moving on to Chapter 4.

What Is Login.gov and Why Does It Matter?

Login.gov is managed by the General Services Administration (GSA) and was built to replace the patchwork of separate login systems maintained by different government agencies. Before Login.gov, you might have needed a different username and password for every federal website you used. Login.gov consolidates it into a single secure account.

For small business owners, Login.gov is the only way to access SAM.gov. Without it, you cannot register your business, update your registration, or renew your annual certification. It is the front door to the entire federal contracting system.

> **Your Login.gov Account Is Personal**
>
> Your Login.gov account is tied to you as an individual, not to your business. Use your personal email address and information when creating it. You will connect it to your business when you register in SAM.gov.

What You Need Before You Start

Creating your Login.gov account takes about 10 minutes if you have these items ready:

- A valid email address that you own and check regularly — this will be your Login.gov username.
- A phone number that can receive text messages or phone calls for two-factor authentication

Optional but recommended: Download an authentication app such as Google Authenticator or Authy for stronger security.

> **Use a Reliable Email**
>
> Use an email address you will have long-term. Your Login.gov account is linked to this email address, and government notifications about your SAM.gov registration will be sent to this address. Avoid using a temporary or work email that you might lose access to.

Step-by-Step: Creating Your Login.gov Account

1	**Go to Login.gov** Open your browser and navigate to login.gov. You will see the Login.gov homepage with options to sign in or create an account.

2	**Click 'Create an account.'** Click the 'Create an account' link below the Sign In button. You will be taken to the account creation page.

3	**Enter your email address** Type in your email address carefully. This will become your Login.gov username. Click Submit to continue.

4	**Check your email and confirm** Login.gov will send a confirmation email to the address you entered. Open the email and click the confirmation link. The link expires after 24 hours, so do this promptly.

5	**Create your password** After confirming your email, you will be prompted to create a password. Login.gov requires a strong password of at least 12 characters. Create something secure and store it in a safe place.

Store Your Password Safely
Use a password manager like LastPass, 1Password, or even a secure note on your phone. You will need this password every time you log into SAM.gov. If you lose it, you can reset it, but it adds unnecessary steps.

6	**Set up two-factor authentication** Two-factor authentication — also called 2FA — adds a second layer of security to your account. Login.gov requires it. You will choose how to receive your second verification code.

Your Two-Factor Authentication Options

Login.gov offers several options for two-factor authentication. Here is what each one means and which we recommend:

Method	How It Works	Recommended?
Authentication App	An app on your phone generates a 6-digit code that refreshes every 30 seconds. Works without cell service.	Yes — **Best Choice**
Text Message (SMS)	Login.gov texts a code to your phone number each time you log in.	Yes — easiest option
Phone Call	Login.gov calls your phone and reads a code aloud.	Acceptable backup
Backup Codes	Login.gov generates 10 one-time codes you save and use if other methods fail.	Save these always
Security Key	A physical USB device you plug into to verify your identity.	Optional advanced option

Save Your Backup Codes
Regardless of which 2FA method you choose, always generate and save your backup codes. If you lose access to your phone or the authentication app, backup codes are the only way to regain access to your account without contacting Login.gov support.

7	**Complete your 2FA setup** Follow the prompts to set up your chosen authentication method. For text message, enter your phone number and verify the code Login.gov sends you. For an authentication app, scan the QR code displayed by Login.gov.

8	**Your account is created** Once 2FA is set up, your Login.gov account is active. You will see a confirmation screen and be directed to your Login.gov account page.

Connecting Your Login.gov Account to SAM.gov

Now that your Login.gov account is created, here is how to connect it to SAM.gov for the first time:

1. Go to sam.gov
2. Click the blue 'Sign In' button in the top right corner.
3. You will be redirected to Login.gov — enter your email and password.
4. Complete your two-factor authentication when prompted.
5. You will be redirected back to SAM.gov, now logged in.
6. The first time you connect, SAM.gov may ask you to agree to its terms of use — read and accept.

Troubleshooting Login.gov Issues

Did not receive the confirmation email

- Check your spam, junk, and promotions folders.
- Add no-reply@login.gov to your contacts and request a new confirmation email.
- Make sure you typed your email address correctly — go back and start over if needed.

Lost access to your two-factor authentication method

- Use one of your saved backup codes to log in.
- If you do not have backup codes, contact Login.gov support at login.gov/help or call 1-844-875-6446.
- Have your email address and account information ready when contacting support.

Forgot your password

- Click 'Forgot password' on the Login.gov sign-in page.
- Enter your email address, and Login.gov will send a reset link.
- Check your email and follow the link to create a new password.

Account locked after too many failed attempts

- Wait 10 minutes and try again.
- If it's still locked, use the "forgot password" option to reset your credentials.

Still need help? Contact Login.gov support at login.gov/help or call 1-844-875-6446.

You have your key. Now let's open the door.

Your Login.gov account is your permanent, secure gateway to the federal digital ecosystem. You will use it every time you log into SAM.gov — to register, to update your information, to renew annually, and to search for contract opportunities.

Take a moment to write down your Login.gov email, password location, and backup codes in a secure place. This is not something you want to scramble to recover when a contract deadline is approaching.

In Chapter 4, we step through the full SAM.gov registration together, section by section. You are ready. Let's go.

Chapter 3 Key Takeaways

- Login.gov is required to access SAM.gov — you cannot register your business without it.
- Your Login.gov account is personal — use your own email address, not a business email, or you might lose it.
- Two-factor authentication is required — text message is the easiest, and the authentication app is the most secure.
- Always save your backup codes — they are your emergency access if you lose your phone.
- The entire setup process takes about 10 minutes if your email and phone are ready.
- For Login.gov support, call 1-844-875-6446 or visit login.gov/help.

CHAPTER FOUR

Step-by-Step SAM.gov Registration: Your Complete Walkthrough

You've made it to the chapter you've been preparing for. With your documents ready and your Login.gov account set up, you're now ready to register your business as a federal contractor on SAM.gov.

Take a moment to breathe before we start. The process can seem overwhelming at first. The screens are full of information, and the language is very official. You might find some questions confusing or start to doubt your answers. That's normal—every business owner who has registered has felt the same way.

You have an advantage with this guide. We'll go through each section together, step by step, so you know what to expect.

Let's get started.

Before You Begin This Chapter

Before you start, be sure you've finished Chapter 2 and have all your documents ready. Don't begin your SAM.gov registration unless you have your EIN, legal business name, NAICS codes, and banking information with you.

Getting Into SAM.gov

Go to sam.gov in your web browser. Click the blue Sign In button at the top right. You'll be sent to Login.gov to sign in. Enter your Login.gov email and password, complete the two-factor authentication, and you'll return to the SAM.gov dashboard.

Navigating the SAM.gov Dashboard

After you log in, the SAM.gov dashboard may seem overwhelming. Here's what you should focus on:

- Look for the "Register / Update Entity" option in the main menu under Entity Information.
- Click "Register New Entity" to begin a fresh registration.
- If you have a previous registration, click "Update Entity" instead.

Pro Tip
SAM.gov will log you out if you're inactive for too long, and you could lose your progress. Save your work often by clicking the Save button at the bottom of each page. You don't have to finish everything at once; you can log back in and pick up where you left off.

Section 1: Core Data

Core Data is the foundation of your SAM.gov registration. This is where you define your business. Take your time here, as mistakes in Core Data are the main reason registrations are rejected.

Entity Information

1	**Legal Business Name** Enter your business name exactly as it appears on your IRS EIN documents. Example: Main Street Consulting LLC. No abbreviations, no variations.

2	**Doing Business As (DBA)** If your business operates under a DBA name, enter it here. If you do not have a DBA, leave this field blank.

3 **Physical Address**

Enter your primary business address. This must be a physical address — not a P.O. Box. A home address is acceptable if that is where your business operates.

4 **Business Start Date**

Enter the date your business was officially formed or registered with your state.

5 **Fiscal Year End Date**

This is the last day of your business's financial year. For most small businesses, this is December 31. Check with your accountant if you are unsure.

Watch Out

SAM.gov will validate your legal business name and EIN against IRS records in real time. If the name does not match exactly what the IRS has on file, you will receive a validation error. See Chapter 5 for how to resolve this.

NAICS Codes

This is where you enter the industry classification codes you identified in Chapter 2. Here is how to enter them correctly:

- Click "Add NAICS Code" and type in your primary NAICS code number.
- Check the box to designate it as your Primary NAICS code.

- Add additional NAICS codes that apply to your business one at a time.
- Review all codes to ensure they accurately reflect your services.

For example, a business offering administrative and consulting services might select codes covering management consulting, office administrative services, and business support services. The goal is to be represented wherever your ideal contracts are posted.

Points of Contact

Enter your points of contact in the Core Data section. SAM.gov requires at least two contacts:

- Government Business Point of Contact: This is the person contracting officers will contact about business opportunities. For most small businesses, this is the owner.
- Electronic Business Point of Contact: The person responsible for managing the SAM.gov registration and receiving system notifications. For most small businesses, this is also the owner.

Section 2: Assertions

The Assertions section is where you tell the federal government important facts about the size and nature of your business. This section determines which set-aside contracts you are eligible to compete for. Read every question carefully.

Business Types

SAM.gov will present a list of business-type designations. Check every box that applies to your business.

- Small Business: check this if you meet the SBA size standards for your NAICS code.
- Woman-Owned Small Business (WOSB): check this if your business is at least 51% owned and controlled by a woman or women.
- Economically Disadvantaged Woman-Owned Small Business (EDWOSB): check this if you qualify under the economic disadvantage criteria.
- Minority Owned Business: check if applicable.
- Veteran Owned Small Business: check if applicable.
- HUBZone Small Business: check whether your business is located in a designated HUBZone.

This Matters More Than You Think

Federal agencies have annual spending goals for contracts awarded to WOSBs, EDWOSBs, veteran-owned businesses, and other designated groups. Checking the right boxes here puts you in front of contracting officers actively seeking to award contracts to businesses like yours.

Size Metrics

SAM.gov will ask for your business size information. You will need to provide:

- Number of employees: average number over the past 12 months.
- Annual revenue: average annual receipts over the past three years.

SBA size standards vary by NAICS code. For most service-based businesses, the standard is based on annual revenue. You can look up the size standard for your specific NAICS code at sba.gov/size-standards.

Disaster Response Registry

SAM.gov will ask if you want to register for the Disaster Response Registry. This is a database of contractors available to provide debris removal, supply distribution, reconstruction, and other services after natural disasters. If this aligns with your business capabilities, check yes. If this does not align with your current services, select no and continue to the next section.

Section 3: Representations and Certifications

This is the longest part of the registration and often causes the most stress for first-time registrants. Take a deep breath. You'll get through it.

Representations and Certifications, often called Reps and Certs, are a set of legal and compliance questions that demonstrate your business's eligibility to work with the federal government.

Read Every Question

Take your time with this section. Every question has legal consequences. If you're unsure about any answer, talk to a business attorney or your local Small Business Development Center (SBDC) before moving forward. Most SBDC services are free.

What You Will Be Asked

While the full list of representations is extensive, here are the categories you will move through:

- FAR Provisions: Federal Acquisition Regulation compliance statements.

- DFARS Provisions: Defense Federal Acquisition Regulation Supplement (applies if you plan to work with the Department of Defense).
- Debarment and Suspension: certifying that your business has not been debarred, suspended, or otherwise excluded from federal contracting.
- Equal Opportunity compliance: certifying adherence to equal employment opportunity requirements.
- Buy American Act: certifications related to domestic manufacturing and products.

How to Move Through This Section

1. Read each question fully before selecting an answer.
2. Most answers for small service-based businesses will be "No" or "Not Applicable."
3. Answer honestly. False certifications are a federal offense.
4. Use the Save button frequently as you work through this section.
5. If a question does not apply to your business, select "Not Applicable" rather than leaving it blank.

> **You Are Not Alone**
>
> The Reps and Certs section is the same for every business registering on SAM.gov. If you are feeling overwhelmed, reach out to your local Procurement Technical Assistance Center (PTAC) or SBDC. They help small businesses complete this section every day at no cost.

Section 4: Final Review and Submission

You're almost done. Before you submit, SAM.gov lets you review your entire registration. Don't skip this step.

Reviewing Your Registration

Check each section again and make sure:

- Your legal business name is spelled correctly and matches your IRS records.
- Your EIN is correct.
- Your physical address is complete and accurate.
- Your NAICS codes reflect your actual business services.
- Your banking information is correct, including your routing number and account number.
- Your points of contact have valid email addresses.
- All business-type designations are checked correctly.

Submitting Your Registration

Once you're sure everything is correct, click the Submit button. SAM.gov will show a confirmation screen with a tracking number. Write this number down or take a screenshot. You'll need it to check your registration status.

What Happens After You Submit

After submission, your registration enters a processing and validation period. Here is what to expect:

1	**IRS Validation (1–2 business days)** SAM.gov validates your EIN and business name against IRS records. You will receive an email notification when this step is complete.

2	**CAGE Code Assignment (1–3 business days)** If this is your first federal registration, the Defense Logistics Agency will assign you a CAGE code — a unique identifier used across federal agencies.

3	**Registration Active (up to 10 business days total)** Once all validations are complete, your registration becomes active. You will receive a confirmation email, and your business will be searchable on SAM.gov.

Check Your Email

SAM.gov sends all status updates to your points of contact's email addresses. Check your inbox — and your spam folder — regularly during the processing period. If you do not receive a confirmation within 10 business days, log back into SAM.gov and check your registration status on the dashboard.

You Did It. Now What?

Finishing your SAM.gov registration is a big achievement. Most small business owners don't get this far. By completing this step, you're ahead of most businesses that could compete for federal contracts but never register.

While you wait for your registration to become active, here is what you can do right now:

- Start working on your capability statement — a one-page document that introduces your business to contracting officers (we cover this in Chapter 9).
- Begin exploring contract opportunities at sam.gov.
- Connect with your local SBDC or PTAC for free guidance on next steps.
- If you are pursuing WOSB or EDWOSB certification, turn to Chapter 7 to get started.

In Chapter 5, we'll cover how to handle errors. Sometimes SAM.gov pushes back, and when that happens, you need to know what to do and how quickly to act. That's coming up next.

Chapter 4 Key Takeaways

- SAM.gov registration has four main sections: Core Data, Assertions, Reps & Certs, and Review & Submit.
- Your legal business name must match IRS records exactly, or your registration will not pass validation.
- Use the callout boxes throughout this chapter to avoid the most common registration mistakes.
- Check all business type designations that apply. WOSB, EDWOSB, and others can help you qualify for set-aside contracts.
- Save your work often. SAM.gov times out, and you could lose your progress.
- After you submit, processing can take up to 10 business days. Keep an eye on your email for status updates.

CHAPTER FIVE

Common Errors and How to Fix Them

Let's be honest. SAM.gov can be tough to use. Since it was designed by the government, it often feels confusing. The error messages are usually unclear, and when something goes wrong, most people aren't sure what to do next.

Here's what you should know: almost every error you see during SAM.gov registration can be fixed. The businesses that give up are usually those that get stuck and don't have anyone to help. You won't be one of them.

This chapter explains the 10 most common errors small business owners encounter during SAM.gov registration, their causes, and how to fix each. Keep this chapter handy. You might not need every tip, but if you run into a problem, you'll know where to look.

Important Note

SAM.gov error messages can sometimes be delayed. If you submit your registration and do not hear back within 2 business days, log in and check your registration status directly on the dashboard. Do not assume everything is fine just because you have not received an error notification.

The Top 10 SAM.gov Registration Errors

1	**IRS Name Mismatch Error** ⚠ Cause: The legal business name you entered in SAM.gov does not exactly match what the IRS has on file for your EIN. Even a small difference — a comma, an ampersand instead of the word "and," or an abbreviation — will trigger this error. ✓ Fix: Log into the IRS website at irs.gov and verify the exact name associated with your EIN. Update your SAM.gov entry to match character-for-character. If your IRS records are outdated or incorrect, you will need to contact the IRS directly to correct them before your registration can proceed.

2	**EIN Validation Failure** ⚠ Cause: SAM.gov could not validate your EIN with the IRS. This can happen if your EIN was recently issued (within the last 2 weeks), if there is a discrepancy in IRS records, or if you entered the number incorrectly. ✓ Fix: Double-check that you entered your EIN correctly with no extra spaces or dashes. If your EIN was recently issued, wait 2 weeks for IRS records to update fully, then try again. If the problem persists, call the IRS TIN Validation line dedicated to SAM.gov at 1-866-255-0654, or the IRS Business & Specialty Tax Line at 1-800-829-4933.

3	**Banking / EFT Verification Error** ⚠ Cause: The bank account or routing number you entered could not be verified. This may be because the account number is incorrect, the routing number does not match your bank's routing number, or the account has restrictions on ACH transfers. ✓ Fix: Verify your routing number by looking at the bottom left of a check from your business account — do not use the routing number from a deposit slip, as these can be different. Call your bank to confirm that your account is set up to accept ACH/EFT transfers. Re-enter your banking information carefully.

4	**DUNS Number / UEI Conflict** ⚠ Cause: If you previously registered on SAM.gov using a DUNS number, you may encounter a conflict when trying to create a new registration or update an existing one tied to the old system. ✓ Fix: Log into SAM.gov and search for your existing entity using your business name or old DUNS number. If a record exists, update that record rather than creating a new one. Contact the SAM.gov Federal Service Desk at fsd.gov if you cannot locate or access your existing record.

5	**Registration Stuck in "Pending" Status** ⚠ Cause: Your registration has been submitted, but has not moved past the pending stage after several business days. An IRS validation hold, a missing document, or a system processing delay usually causes this. ✓ Fix: Log into SAM.gov and check your registration status. If it shows "Pending IRS Validation" after more than 5 business days, contact the IRS to confirm that your EIN and business name are in their system. If it shows "Pending Validation" without a specific reason, contact the SAM.gov Federal Service Desk for assistance.

6	**Duplicate Entity Record** ⚠ Cause: SAM.gov has detected that an entity with your EIN or business name already exists in the system. This often happens when a previous registration was started but not completed, or when someone else in your organization began one. ✓ Fix: Search SAM.gov for your business name and EIN to locate the existing record. If you can access it, continue updating that record. If you cannot access it because it is associated with a different Login.gov account, contact the SAM.gov Federal Service Desk with proof of business ownership to have the record transferred or corrected.

7	**CAGE Code Not Assigned** ⚠ Cause: After your registration was approved, you did not receive a CAGE code assignment. This sometimes happens if there is a processing delay with the Defense Logistics Agency or if your registration information requires manual review. ✓ Fix: CAGE code assignment typically takes 1 to 3 business days after your registration is approved. If you have not received your CAGE code after 5 business days, contact the Defense Logistics Agency directly at dla.mil or call 1-877-352-2255 or email dlacontactcenter@dla.mil.

8	**Address Validation Error** ⚠ Cause: SAM.gov could not validate your physical business address. This can happen if your address does not match USPS records, if you used abbreviations the system does not recognize, or if your address is in a rural area that is not fully indexed. ✓ Fix: Visit usps.com and use the address verification tool to confirm how the USPS formats your address. Enter your address in SAM.gov exactly as USPS formats it. If you are in a rural area with an address that USPS cannot verify, contact the SAM.gov Federal Service Desk for guidance on alternative address entry options.

9	**Registration Expired Due to Missed Annual Renewal** ⚠ Cause: Your SAM.gov registration expired because you did not complete the annual renewal within the required timeframe. An expired registration makes your business ineligible for federal contracts until it is renewed. ✓ Fix: Log into SAM.gov and click "Renew Entity." Review and update all sections as needed, then resubmit. Renewals typically process faster than new registrations. Set a calendar reminder 60 days before your annual expiration date to avoid this situation in the future.

10	**Notarized Letter Required** ⚠ Cause: SAM.gov has flagged your registration and is requesting a notarized letter to verify your entity information. This is more common among sole proprietors or businesses with minimal IRS records. ✓ Fix: SAM.gov will send instructions to your points of contact's email with specific details on what the notarized letter must include. Follow the instructions exactly. The letter must be notarized by a licensed notary public and submitted through the method specified in the email. Processing resumes once the letter is received and reviewed.

Who to Contact for Help

If you've tried everything you can and still need help, here are the official resources you can use:

Resource	Contact / Website	Best For
SAM.gov Federal Service Desk	fsd.gov | Mon-Fri 8am-8pm EST	Registration issues, locked accounts, duplicate records
IRS Business Tax Line	irs.gov | 1-800-829-4933	EIN validation, name mismatch, IRS record corrections
Defense Logistics Agency	dla.mil | 1-877-352-2255 | dlacontactcenter@dla.mil	CAGE code issues
Small Business Development Center (SBDC)	americassbdc.org	Free guidance on completing registration and Reps & Certs
APEX Accelerator (formerly PTAC)	aptac-us.org	Free local support for government contracting readiness

Tips for Faster Error Resolution

When you reach out to any of these agencies for help, come prepared. The more information you have ready, the faster your issue will be resolved.

- Have your SAM.gov tracking number ready — the one you received when you submitted your registration.
- Know your EIN and legal business name exactly as entered.
- Take screenshots of any error messages before you close them.
- Write down the date and time you first encountered the error.

- Note any reference numbers or case numbers given to you during support calls.
- Follow up in writing by email whenever possible, so you have a paper trail.

Document Everything

Government systems can be slow and support staff change. Every time you call or email about an error, write down the date, the name of the person you spoke with, and what they told you. If you have to escalate, this documentation is invaluable.

Errors Are Part of the Process — Not the End of It

Here's something to remember: running into an error on SAM.gov doesn't mean you did anything wrong. The system is complicated, the checks are strict, and even experienced contractors sometimes have problems. What matters is not letting an error stop you.

Every error in this chapter has been solved by small business owners just like you. With the right information and some persistence, your registration will go through. When it does, you'll have access to the largest procurement marketplace in the world.

Keep going. Next up is Chapter 6, where we'll take a closer look at your UEI number and how you can use it to help your business.

Chapter 5 Key Takeaways

- Almost every SAM.gov error has a solution — don't give up when one appears.
- IRS name mismatch is the most common error — verify your exact IRS business name before registering.
- Screenshot every error message before closing it — you will need it when seeking help.
- If SAM.gov requests a notarized letter, follow the emailed instructions exactly and submit through the specified method.
- The SAM.gov Federal Service Desk, IRS, SBDC, and APEX Accelerator (formerly PTAC) are all free resources available to help you.
- Document every support interaction with dates, names, and reference numbers.

CHAPTER SIX

Understanding Your UEI Number: Your Federal Business Identity

You have finished registering your business, and it is now in the system. Somewhere on your SAM.gov dashboard, there is a 12-character code that many small business owners see once and then forget.

But forgetting that code is a mistake.

Your Unique Entity Identifier, or UEI, is one of the most important numbers your business will ever receive. The federal government uses it to identify you for every agency, contract, and grant application. Knowing your UEI, where to find it, and how to use it properly can mean the difference between winning an opportunity and being disqualified for a minor mistake.

This chapter explains everything you need to know so you will not be left guessing.

What Is the UEI and Where Did It Come From?

The Unique Entity Identifier is a 12-character code composed of letters and numbers. SAM.gov assigns it to every business that registers in the system. In April 2022, it replaced the DUNS number, which was managed by Dun & Bradstreet, as the official federal identifier.

For almost 30 years, the DUNS number was the main identifier for federal contractors and grant recipients. The government chose to manage the identifier itself, eliminating the need for a private company and simplifying things for small businesses. Now, the UEI is free, government-managed, and automatically issued to you when you register on SAM.gov.

Your DUNS Number Is No Longer Valid

As of April 4, 2022, the DUNS number is no longer accepted for federal contracting or grant applications. If you have an older registration that referenced your DUNS number, your UEI has already been assigned and is visible in your SAM.gov entity record. The DUNS number plays no role in the federal contracting process going forward.

What Does a UEI Look Like?

A UEI is exactly 12 characters and uses both letters and numbers.

It looks like this:

Example UEI Format:

A B 1 C D 2 E F 3 G H 4

12 characters — letters and numbers — unique to your business entity.

SAM.gov created your UEI when you registered, and it stays linked to your business. It only changes if you register a new business entity.

Where to Find Your UEI

There are three places you can find your UEI:

1. In Your SAM.gov Entity Record

This is the most reliable place to find your UEI. Log in to sam.gov, go to your entity registration, and you will see your UEI at the top of your record. It is also in your registration confirmation emails from SAM.gov.

2. Through the SAM.gov Public Search

Anyone can find a business's UEI using the SAM.gov public database. Go to sam.gov, click Search, and look up your business by name or location. Your entity record will display your UEI to anyone. Contracting officers and prime contractors use this to check your registration status.

3. On Your Printed Registration Documents

If you saved or printed your SAM.gov registration confirmation, your UEI is at the top of that document. Keep a copy in your business files so you can find it easily when needed.

Write It Down and Keep It Accessible

Add your UEI to your business contact sheet, your capability statement, and any government contracting templates you use. You will be asked for it frequently, and it is important to have it immediately accessible.

UEI vs. DUNS vs. CAGE Code — What Is the Difference?

If you have looked into government contracting, you have likely seen all three of these terms. Here is a simple explanation of each and how they are connected:

Feature	UEI	DUNS (retired)	CAGE Code
Managed by	SAM.gov (GSA)	Dun & Bradstreet (retired)	Defense Logistics Agency
Length	12 characters	9 digits	5 characters
Cost	Free	Was free	Free
Currently required	✓ Yes	✗ No — retired 2022	✓ Yes for DoD contracts
Assigned when	During SAM registration	✗ No — retired 2022	After SAM registration is approved
Used for	All federal contracting & grants	✗ No — retired 2022	DoD and defense-related work
Changes	Stays with the entity	✗ No — retired 2022	Stays with the entity at the location

You Need Both UEI and CAGE

For most federal contracts, especially those with the Department of Defense, you will need both your UEI and your CAGE code. Your UEI identifies your entity in SAM.gov. Your CAGE code identifies your physical business location within the Defense Acquisition System. Both are assigned through the SAM.gov registration process.

How to Use Your UEI

Your UEI is more than just a number to store away. It is an active key for government contracting. Here is where and how you will use it:

On Proposals and Bids

Every federal proposal, bid, or quote you submit will require your UEI. Contracting officers check it to make sure your SAM.gov registration is active before awarding a contract. If your registration has expired or your UEI does not match an active registration, your bid may be automatically disqualified.

On Grant Applications

Federal grant applications on Grants.gov and other sites also require your UEI. The same rules apply: your SAM.gov registration must be active, and your UEI must match the one in your entity record.

On Your Capability Statement

A capability statement is a one-page marketing document you give to contracting officers to introduce your business. Your UEI should be listed in the company information section, along with your CAGE code, NAICS codes, and business certifications. We will discuss capability statements in more detail in Chapter 9.

On Subcontracting Agreements

If you work as a subcontractor for a prime contractor, you will need to give them your UEI. The prime uses it to check your registration and report your role in their subcontracting plan. Always keep your SAM.gov registration active when seeking subcontracting work.

When Registering on Other Government Platforms

Many federal agency procurement sites, state government systems, and grant platforms will ask for your UEI when you register or apply. If you have your UEI memorized or can access it quickly, these steps will go much faster.

> **Keep Your Registration Active**
>
> Your UEI is only useful if your SAM.gov registration is active. An expired registration means your UEI will show as inactive when contracting officers look you up. We cover how to keep your registration current in Chapter 8.

Verifying Your UEI Status

Before you send any proposal or application, it is a good idea to check that your UEI is active and your SAM.gov registration is up to date. Here is how you can do that:

1. Go to sam.gov
2. Click on Search in the top navigation.
3. Select Entity Information from the search options.
4. Search for your business by name or enter your UEI directly.
5. Your entity record will show your registration status. Look for the word Active in green.

Check Before Every Submission

Make it a habit to verify your SAM.gov status before submitting any proposal, application, or bid. A registration that expired yesterday can cost you a contract today. This check takes less than two minutes and can save you from a disqualifying mistake.

Pro Tip: Make sure your registration expires at least 30 days from the date you submit a bid.

Your UEI and Business Changes

Sometimes, changes in your business can affect how your UEI is linked to your entity record. Here is what you need to know:

If You Change Your Business Name

Changing your legal business name does not change your UEI. Your UEI stays the same, but you need to update your SAM.gov registration with the new name. Make sure the update matches your new IRS records exactly.

If You Change Your Business Address

Changing your address does not affect your UEI. Update your SAM.gov registration with the new address and make sure it passes USPS validation. Remember, your CAGE code is linked to your physical location, so moving may result in a new CAGE code.

If You Change Your Business Structure

Major changes to your business, such as switching from a sole proprietorship to an LLC or changing your EIN, may require you to register a new entity in SAM.gov. This would give you a new UEI. Contact the SAM.gov Federal Service Desk at fsd.gov before making major changes to ensure you understand how they will affect your registration.

If You Have Multiple Business Locations

Each separate legal entity or business location that registers in SAM.gov receives its own UEI. If your business operates multiple locations under different legal entities, each entity will have its own UEI and its own SAM.gov registration to keep up to date.

Your UEI Is Your Federal Identity — Protect It

Your UEI is publicly visible in the SAM.gov database. Contractors, agencies, and anyone else can search for it and see your business information. This is intentional because it helps keep government contracting transparent.

This means that the information linked to your UEI, such as your business name, address, certifications, and registration status, constitutes your public federal identity. Keep this information accurate and up to date so it always shows the most current and truthful details about your business.

In Chapter 7, we will cover WOSB and EDWOSB certification. These designations can make your UEI even more valuable in the federal marketplace.

Turn the page — Chapter 7 is your next step.

Chapter 6 Key Takeaways

- The UEI replaced the DUNS number in April 2022 — the DUNS number is no longer used for federal contracting.
- Your UEI is 12 characters long, free, and automatically assigned when you register in SAM.gov.
- You will use your UEI on every proposal, grant application, capability statement, and subcontracting agreement.
- Your UEI and CAGE code work together — both are needed for most federal contracting opportunities.
- Always verify your SAM.gov registration is active before submitting any bid or application.
- Business name and address changes do not change your UEI — but structural changes or new EINs may require a new registration.

CHAPTER SEVEN

WOSB and EDWOSB Certification: Unlocking Set-Aside Contracts

This chapter is for women business owners. If you run your own small business, the information here could make a big difference for your company.

The federal government must award some of its contracts to Women-Owned Small Businesses and Economically Disadvantaged Women-Owned Small Businesses. These are called set-aside contracts. Only businesses like yours can win them, not larger competitors.

In FY 2023, the federal government awarded a record $178.6 billion in contracts to small businesses, exceeding its 23% small business contracting goal for the year. Of that amount, $30.9 billion went specifically to Women-Owned Small Businesses — the highest dollar amount ever awarded to WOSBs — according to the SBA's annual Small Business Procurement Scorecard.

This chapter will explain how to get certified, what certification means for your business, and how to find these opportunities.

This Chapter Applies to You If...
Your business is at least 51% owned, operated, and controlled by one or more women who are U.S. citizens, and your business qualifies as a small business under SBA size standards for your primary NAICS code.

What Is WOSB Certification?

WOSB means Women-Owned Small Business. This federal certification lets your business compete for set-aside contracts in industries where women are underrepresented.

The SBA, or Small Business Administration, created the WOSB program to give women entrepreneurs a fair chance in the federal marketplace. When a contract is marked as a WOSB set-aside, only certified WOSBs can compete for it.

WOSB Eligibility Requirements

To qualify as a WOSB, your business must meet all of the following criteria:

- Your business must be a small business as defined by SBA size standards for your primary NAICS code.
- Your business must be at least 51% unconditionally and directly owned by one or more women who are U.S. citizens.
- The woman or women owners must control the management and daily business operations.
- The woman or women owners must hold the highest officer position in the company.
- The woman or women owners must make long-term and day-to-day business decisions.

What Does "Control" Mean?

The SBA takes control seriously. It is not enough to simply own 51% of the business. The woman owner must actually be in charge — making strategic decisions, managing operations, and holding the highest officer position. A business where a man makes the real decisions but a woman holds the ownership title will not qualify.

What Is EDWOSB Certification?

EDWOSB stands for Economically Disadvantaged Woman-Owned Small Business. This is a higher level of WOSB certification and comes with extra set-aside opportunities. An EDWOSB can compete for all WOSB set-asides, as well as those set aside for economically disadvantaged women.

To qualify as an EDWOSB, you need to meet all the WOSB requirements and also show that you are economically disadvantaged based on your personal finances.

EDWOSB Economic Disadvantage Requirements

The SBA looks at three financial factors to decide if you are economically disadvantaged:

- Personal net worth must be less than $850,000 — excluding the value of your primary residence and your ownership interest in the business.

- Adjusted gross income averaged over the three most recent tax years must be $400,000 or less.

- Total fair market value of all assets must be $6.5 million or less, excluding the value of your primary residence and your ownership interest in the business.

> **Check Your Numbers**
>
> These thresholds are based on your personal finances, not your business finances. Many women who assume they do not qualify are surprised to find they do. Run through these numbers carefully before assuming EDWOSB is out of reach.

WOSB vs. EDWOSB at a Glance

Requirement	**WOSB**	**EDWOSB**
51% woman owned	✓ Required	✓ Required
Women control operations	✓ Required	✓ Required
U.S. citizen owner	✓ Required	✓ Required
SBA small business size	✓ Required	✓ Required
Personal net worth limit	Not required	Under $850,000
Personal income limit	Not required	$400,000 avg or less
Total assets limit	Not required	$6.5 million or less
WOSB set-aside eligible	✓ Yes	✓ Yes
EDWOSB set-aside eligible	✗ No	✓ Yes

How to Get Certified: Your Step-by-Step Path

Since 2020, the SBA has required all businesses seeking WOSB or EDWOSB status to be certified either directly by the SBA or through an SBA-approved third-party certifier. Self-certification is no longer sufficient for most set-aside contracts.

Option 1: SBA Direct Certification (Recommended)

The SBA offers free direct certification through the MySBA Certification portal. This is the most accepted and affordable option.

1	**Create or log in to your MySBA account** Go to certify.sba.gov and create an account or log in with your existing credentials.

2	**Complete your SAM.gov registration first** You must have an active SAM.gov registration before applying for WOSB/EDWOSB certification. Your UEI number will be required during the application.

3	**Select WOSB or EDWOSB certification** Choose the appropriate certification level based on your eligibility. You can apply for EDWOSB directly — you do not need to get WOSB first.

4	**Complete the application and upload documents** The portal will walk you through a series of questions and ask you to upload supporting documentation. See the document checklist below.

5	**Submit and await review** SBA reviewers will evaluate your application. Processing time varies but typically takes 30 to 90 days. You will receive notifications through your MySBA portal.

6	**Certification is granted** Once approved, your WOSB or EDWOSB status will automatically be reflected on SAM.gov. Contracting officers can see your certification when searching for eligible vendors.

It Is Free SBA direct certification through the MySBA portal is completely free. You do not need to pay anyone to certify your business. If someone is asking you to pay for SBA WOSB certification, that is not the SBA direct path.

Option 2: Third-Party Certifiers

The SBA has approved several third-party organizations to certify WOSBs and EDWOSBs. These groups usually charge a fee, but they might process your application faster or give you extra help.

SBA-approved third-party certifiers include organizations such as the Women's Business Enterprise National Council (WBENC), the National Women Business Owners Corporation (NWBOC), and others listed on the SBA website at sba.gov/federal-contracting/contracting-assistance-programs/women-owned-small-business-federal-contracting-program.

Documents You Will Need

Whether you certify through the SBA or a third-party certifier, you will need to collect documents that show your ownership, control, and eligibility. Here is what to prepare:

For All WOSB Applicants

- Business formation documents — Articles of Incorporation, Articles of Organization, or Partnership Agreement.
- Operating Agreement or Bylaws showing ownership percentages.
- Signed and dated Meeting Minutes demonstrating current operating practices, including evidence of officer elections, adoption of bylaws, voting agreements, and business decisions.
- Business licenses and any professional licenses required to operate.
- Most recent federal business tax return.
- Proof of U.S. citizenship for all women owners — passport, birth certificate, or naturalization certificate.
- IRS SS4 letter or 1040 Schedule C with the correct business name and EIN — used to verify your Taxpayer Identification Number.
- Resume or biography demonstrating the woman owner's management experience and control of the business.
- Organizational chart for a business with employees and reporting structure.
- Fictitious Name Certificate or Certificate of Trade Name — if your business operates under a DBA.

Additional Documents for EDWOSB Applicants

- Personal financial statements for all women owners claiming economic disadvantage.

- The three most recent personal federal tax returns for each woman owner, including all schedules and attachments.
- W-2 statements for the last three years — if you filed jointly with a spouse, include your spouse's W-2 as well.
- Documentation of all personal assets, including real estate, investment accounts, retirement accounts, vehicles, and other property.
- Documentation of any liabilities, including mortgages, loans, and other debts.
- Evidence of any asset transfers made to immediate family members in the last two years below fair market value.

Start Gathering Now

Open a folder — physical or digital — and begin collecting these documents today. The application will not wait for you to go searching. Missing a single document is the most common reason applications stall.

The owners who move through certification the fastest are the ones who show up prepared.

Finding WOSB and EDWOSB Set-Aside Contracts

Once you are certified, you need to know how to find the opportunities that are reserved for you. Here is how to search for WOSB and EDWOSB set-aside contracts on SAM.gov:

1. Go to sam.gov and click on Contract Opportunities.

2. In the search filters, look for the Set-Aside Type filter.

3. Select "Woman Owned Small Business" and/or "EDWOSB" from the dropdown.

4. Add your NAICS code to narrow results to your industry.

5. Review active opportunities and set up email alerts for new postings that match your criteria.

Set Up Alerts
SAM.gov allows you to save searches and receive email notifications when new contracts matching your criteria are posted. Set this up the day your certification is approved so you never miss an opportunity.

Understanding Set-Aside Contract Language

When reviewing contract opportunities, look for these terms in the solicitation to identify set-aside contracts:

- Set-Aside: Total Small Business — open to all small businesses.

- Set-Aside: WOSB — restricted to certified Woman Owned Small Businesses.

- Set-Aside: EDWOSB — restricted to certified Economically Disadvantaged Woman Owned Small Businesses.

- Set-Aside: Partial — a portion of the contract is set aside while the rest is open competition.

Maintaining Your Certification

WOSB and EDWOSB certifications are not one-time events. You have ongoing responsibilities to maintain your certification in good standing.

- Annual recertification: You must recertify your WOSB or EDWOSB status every year through the MySBA portal.
- Notify the SBA of any changes: If your ownership structure, size, or financial status changes in a way that could affect your eligibility, you must let the SBA know.
- Keep your SAM.gov registration current: Your SAM.gov registration must stay active for your certification to be recognized by contracting officers.
- Respond to program examinations: The SBA randomly examines certified businesses to check ongoing eligibility. If you are selected, respond quickly and provide all requested information.

Set Annual Reminders

Put your WOSB/EDWOSB recertification date and your SAM.gov renewal date in your calendar right now. Letting either one lapse can make you ineligible for contracts you are otherwise perfectly qualified to win.

You Earned Your Seat at This Table

WOSB and EDWOSB certification is not a shortcut or a handout. It recognizes that women business owners have historically faced barriers in the federal marketplace, and it has implemented a deliberate policy to open those doors.

You have built a real business. You have registered, learned the system, and positioned yourself to compete. Certification is the next step to help the right contracting officers find you when they need your services.

Get certified. Your contracts are waiting.

Chapter 7 Key Takeaways

- WOSB and EDWOSB certifications unlock set-aside contracts that are off-limits to non-certified competitors.
- EDWOSB carries additional eligibility and is worth pursuing if you meet the personal financial thresholds.
- SBA direct certification through certify.sba.gov is free and the most widely accepted path.
- You must have an active SAM.gov registration before applying for WOSB/EDWOSB certification.
- Gather your ownership and financial documents before starting the application to avoid delays.
- Recertify annually and keep your SAM.gov registration active to maintain your eligibility.

CHAPTER EIGHT

Maintaining and Renewing Your Registration: Staying Active and Eligible

Getting registered on SAM.gov is a big achievement. But most guides leave out an important detail: registration is not a one-time task. It is something you need to keep up with regularly.

Your SAM.gov registration expires every 365 days. If you let it lapse, your business becomes ineligible for federal contracts and grants until you renew. Contracting officers cannot award to an expired entity. Grant administrators cannot fund one. And in some cases, an expired registration can disqualify a bid you have already submitted.

The good news is that keeping your registration up to date is easy once you know the steps and timing. This chapter will show you how to stay active, stay compliant, and avoid missing a renewal.

Mark Your Calendar Right Now

Your SAM.gov registration expires exactly 365 days from the date it was last activated or renewed. Before you read another word of this chapter, log into SAM.gov, find your expiration date, and add a reminder to your calendar for 60 days before that date. Do it now. We will be here when you get back.

Understanding Your Registration Expiration

Every SAM.gov entity registration has an expiration date. You can find yours by logging into SAM.gov and viewing your entity record. The expiration date is displayed prominently at the top of your registration summary.

SAM.gov will email your points of contact as your expiration date gets closer. Still, do not count only on these reminders. Emails can end up in spam, go to old addresses, or get missed when things are busy. Set up your own reminder system, too.

What Happens When Your Registration Expires

The moment your registration expires, the following happens immediately:

- Your entity record status changes from Active to Expired in the SAM.gov public database.
- Contracting officers searching for eligible vendors will not see your business in filtered results.
- Any bids or proposals you submit with an expired registration can be rejected.
- Your WOSB or EDWOSB certification status becomes invalid until renewed.
- Federal grant applications requiring an active SAM.gov registration will be ineligible.

Expired Does Not Mean Deleted

An expired registration does not erase your entity record. Your UEI, CAGE code, and registration history remain intact. You simply need to renew to reactivate your Active status. The renewal process is faster than the original registration.

How to Renew Your Registration

Renewing your SAM.gov registration is simple and uses the same login steps as your first registration. Here is what to do:

1. Log in to SAM.gov using your Login.gov credentials.
2. Navigate to your entity record from your workspace dashboard.
3. Click the 'Renew' button on your entity registration.
4. Check each part of your registration for accuracy and update anything that has changed.
5. Pay special attention to your points of contact, email addresses, NAICS codes, and banking information.
6. Review and resubmit your Representations and Certifications.
7. Submit your renewal.
8. Processing can take up to 10 business days, but renewals are often completed faster than new registrations.

Review Everything During Renewal

Do not just click through the renewal without reading. Your business may have changed since your last registration — new services, new address, updated banking, staff changes. Renewal is your annual opportunity to make sure your federal profile accurately reflects your current business.

What to Update During Renewal

Treat your annual renewal as a chance to review your entire SAM.gov profile. Here is a checklist of what to look over and update if needed:

Core Data

- Legal business name: Make sure it still matches your IRS records exactly.
- Physical address: Update this if you have moved.
- Mailing address: Update if it is different from your physical address.
- Phone number and website.
- Fiscal year-end date: Update if your financial year has changed.

Points of Contact

- Government Business POC: Make sure the name, title, email, and phone number are current.
- Electronic Business POC: Make sure the email is active and checked regularly.

- Remove any contacts who are no longer with your business.

NAICS Codes

- Review your primary NAICS code: Is it still the best fit for your main service?
- Add new NAICS codes if you now offer more services.
- Remove any codes that no longer match your business.

Banking Information

- Verify your routing number is still correct.
- Verify your account number is still correct.
- Update if you have changed banks or accounts since your last registration.

Business Type Designations

- Check that your small business size status is still correct based on your current revenue and number of employees.
- Update your WOSB or EDWOSB status if your ownership or financial situation has changed.
- Add any new designations that now apply, such as veteran-owned or HUBZone.

Banking Updates Are Critical

If your bank account has changed since your last registration and you receive a contract payment, it will be sent to the old account on file. Update your banking information at every renewal and whenever your account changes during the year.

Updating Your Registration Between Renewals

You do not need to wait for your annual renewal to update your SAM.gov registration. Update it whenever your business information changes. Here is how:

1. Log in to SAM.gov with your Login.gov credentials.
2. Navigate to your entity record.
3. Click 'Update' on your entity registration.
4. Make the necessary changes to the relevant section.
5. Submit the update.
6. Allow up to 3 to 5 business days for the update to process and appear in the public database.

Changes That Require Immediate Updates

- Business name change — must match updated IRS records.
- Physical address change.
- Banking information change.

- Change in ownership that affects WOSB or EDWOSB eligibility.
- Key personnel changes in your points of contact.
- Business structure change, such as converting from a sole proprietorship to an LLC.

Do Not Wait for Renewal
If your banking information changes, update SAM.gov immediately — not at your next renewal. The same applies to ownership changes that affect your certifications. Waiting can result in misdirected payments or certification issues.

Your Annual Registration Renewal Timeline

Use this timeline as a guide to stay up to date on SAM.gov maintenance throughout the year. Adjust the months to fit your own expiration date.

Timing	Action	Priority
60 days out	Log into SAM.gov and review your full entity record for any needed updates	Critical
60 days out	Confirm that your points of contact's email addresses are active and monitored	Critical
45 days out	Begin your renewal process — do not wait until the last week	Critical
45 days out	Update NAICS codes, banking info, and business designations as needed	Important

Timing	Action	Priority
30 days out	Submit your renewal if not already done	Critical
30 days out	Verify your WOSB/EDWOSB recertification is also current	Important
14 days out	Confirm renewal has been processed, and the status shows Active	Critical
14 days out	Contact SAM.gov Federal Service Desk if still showing Pending	Important
Anytime	Update registration immediately if banking, address, or ownership changes	Critical
Annually	Review and update your NAICS codes to reflect current services	Recommended
Annually	Request a free capability statement review from your local APEX Accelerator	Recommended

Setting Up Reminders That Actually Work

The main reason SAM.gov registrations expire is that business owners forget to renew them. Life gets busy. Here are the best reminder strategies:

Calendar Reminders

- Set a repeating annual reminder 60 days before your expiration date.
- Set a second reminder 30 days before as a backup.

- Use Google Calendar, Outlook, or your phone calendar, whichever you check every day.

Email Notifications from SAM.gov

- SAM.gov sends renewal reminder emails at 60, 30, and 15 days before expiration.
- Make sure your points of contact's email addresses are up to date and actively monitored.
- Add no-reply@sam.gov to your safe sender's list so reminder emails do not end up in spam.

Business Calendar Integration

- Add your SAM.gov expiration date to your business compliance calendar, along with your state registration renewal, business license renewal, and tax deadlines.
- Give it the same priority as any other legal business deadline.

Build It Into Your Business Routine

The most successful government contractors treat SAM.gov maintenance like they treat paying their business taxes — it is a non-negotiable annual task that gets scheduled and handled on time, every time. Make it part of your standard business operations calendar, and it will never catch you off guard.

Staying Compliant Year-Round

In addition to the annual renewal, staying compliant with SAM.gov means keeping your information accurate year-round. Here is a simple quarterly check-in routine to keep your registration up to date:

Quarter	Quick Check-In Tasks
Q1	Log in and confirm Active status. Review points of contact. Confirm banking information is current.
Q2	Review NAICS codes against current service offerings. Check expiration date and note days remaining.
Q3	Begin renewal process if expiration is within 90 days. Confirm WOSB/EDWOSB status is current.
Q4	Complete annual renewal if not already done. Update any changes from the past year. Set reminders for next year.

You Built This. Now Protect It.

Your SAM.gov registration took real effort. You spent time, gathered documents, and showed patience and persistence. Letting it expire puts all that work at risk for a reason you can easily avoid.

See your annual renewal as a business investment, not a burden. It takes just 30 minutes a year to keep your chance at federal contracts open. The businesses that win contracts are the ones that stay ready, stay compliant, and never give a contracting officer a reason to look elsewhere.

In Chapter 9, we move from maintaining your registration to putting it to use. You will learn how to find contract opportunities, use the search tools, and position your business to win. That is where the real excitement begins.

Chapter 8 Key Takeaways

- Your SAM.gov registration expires every 365 days — an expired registration makes you ineligible for contracts and grants.
- Begin your renewal at least 45 days before expiration to allow time for processing.
- Use renewal as your annual audit — review and update all sections, including NAICS codes, banking, and contacts.
- Update your registration immediately when banking, address, or ownership changes — do not wait for renewal.
- Set calendar reminders at 60 days and 30 days before your expiration date as your personal backup system.
- A quarterly check-in routine keeps your registration accurate and your business ready to win year-round.

CHAPTER NINE

Finding Opportunities After Registration: Putting Your SAM.gov Registration to Work

Congratulations! After all your preparation and paperwork, your business is now officially registered and listed on the world's largest procurement marketplace. Your UEI is active, your certifications are set, and your business can be seen by more than 400 federal agencies and thousands of contracting officers.

Now what?

Registration is not the finish line; it is the starting point. The businesses that succeed in federal contracting use their SAM.gov registration as a tool, not just a certificate to display. This chapter will help you go from simply being registered to being ready to win contracts.

We will cover how to search for contract opportunities, understand what you find, position your business with a capability statement, and start building the relationships that lead to contracts. By the end of this chapter, you will have a clear action plan for your first 90 days as a registered federal contractor.

Understanding the Federal Contracting Marketplace

Each year, the federal government spends over $600 billion on goods and services. This includes everything from office supplies and IT services to construction, consulting, and administrative support.

This money is spread across hundreds of federal agencies, each with its own needs, budgets, and procurement processes. As a small business owner, your job is to find out which agencies need your services and get your business in front of the people who make purchasing decisions.

> **Small Business Goals Work in Your Favor**
>
> By law, the federal government sets annual small business contracting goals. The overall government-wide goal is that 23% of all federal prime contract dollars go to small businesses. Within that, there are separate goals for WOSBs, veteran-owned businesses, HUBZone businesses, and 8(a) participants. Agencies are measured on whether they meet these goals, which means contracting officers are actively looking for qualified small businesses like yours.

Searching for Contract Opportunities on SAM.gov

SAM.gov is the official database for federal contract opportunities. All federal contracts above a certain amount are posted here. Learning to search SAM.gov well is one of the most valuable skills you can have as a government contractor.

Getting to the Contract Opportunities Search

1. Go to sam.gov
2. Click on Contract Opportunities in the top navigation bar.
3. You will land on the main search page for federal solicitations.

How to Search Effectively

If you search too broadly, you will get thousands of results. Here is how to narrow them down to the opportunities that fit your business best:

1	**Search by NAICS Code** Enter your primary NAICS code in the search bar. This immediately filters results to contracts in your industry. You can search multiple NAICS codes by running separate searches.

2	**Filter by Set-Aside Type** In the left filter panel, select your applicable set-aside designation — WOSB, EDWOSB, Small Business, or others. This shows only the contracts reserved for businesses with your certification.

3	**Filter by Place of Performance** If you prefer local or regional work, filter by state or city. Many service contracts prefer or require local vendors.

4	**Filter by Agency** If you have identified specific agencies whose missions align with your services, filter by agency to see their active opportunities.

5	**Filter by Contract Type** Filter by opportunity type — Solicitation, Sources Sought, Presolicitation, or Award Notice. Sources Sought notices are particularly valuable for new contractors — see the section below.

Start With Sources Sought Notices

Sources Sought notices are market research postings in which agencies explore whether qualified small businesses exist for a future requirement. Responding to Sources Sought notices does not commit you to anything — but it gets your business in front of the contracting officer before the formal solicitation is even released. This is one of the most underused strategies by new government contractors.

Understanding Set-Aside Contract Types

When you filter by set-aside type, you will see several designations. Here is a reference guide to the most common ones and who qualifies:

Code	Set-Aside Type	Who Qualifies
SBA	Total Small Business Set-Aside	Any business that meets SBA small business size standards for the applicable NAICS code
WOSB	Woman-Owned Small Business	Certified WOSBs in industries where women are underrepresented in federal contracting
EDWOSB	Economically Disadvantaged WOSB	Certified EDWOSBs meeting personal financial thresholds — the most competitive set-aside for women
SDVOSB	Service-Disabled Veteran Owned	Businesses at least 51% owned by a service-disabled veteran
VOSB	Veteran Owned Small Business	Businesses at least 51% owned and controlled by a veteran

Code	Set-Aside Type	Who Qualifies
HUBZone	Historically Underutilized Business Zone	Businesses located in and employing residents of designated HUBZone areas
8(a)	8(a) Business Development Program	Businesses owned by socially and economically disadvantaged individuals, SBA-certified

Reading a Contract Opportunity

When you find a promising opportunity, click the listing to open the full solicitation package. Here is how to quickly decide if an opportunity is worth pursuing:

Key Information to Review First

- Response deadline — do you have enough time to prepare a competitive response?
- Place of performance — is the work location feasible for your business?
- Contract type — is it a fixed price, time and materials, or cost reimbursement contract?
- Estimated value — is the contract size appropriate for your business capacity?
- Set-aside type — are you eligible based on your certifications?
- NAICS code — does it match your primary or secondary NAICS codes?

- Statement of Work — do your services genuinely match what is being requested?

Be Honest With Yourself

Not every opportunity is the right fit. Pursue contracts where you can genuinely deliver excellent results. A strong performance on a smaller contract builds your past performance record far more effectively than a poor performance on a larger one you were not ready for.

Setting Up Opportunity Alerts

Manually searching SAM.gov every day is not sustainable. Set up saved searches and email alerts so new opportunities come directly to your inbox.

1. Run a search using your preferred filters — NAICS code, set-aside type, agency, etc.

2. Click the Save Search button at the top right of the results page.

3. Give your saved search a name you will recognize.

4. Choose how often you want to get email notifications. Daily alerts are best if you are actively looking for opportunities.

5. Click Save. SAM.gov will email you whenever new opportunities match your criteria.

Create Multiple Saved Searches

Set up separate saved searches for each of your NAICS codes, for WOSB set-asides specifically, and for any target agencies you have identified. This ensures you never miss an opportunity that fits your business.

Your Capability Statement: Your Federal Business Card

Before you respond to any solicitation, you need a capability statement. This one-page document introduces your business to contracting officers and prime contractors. It is the most important marketing document you will create as a government contractor.

A good capability statement quickly explains who you are, what you do, and why the government should work with you. It should take less than a minute to read.

What Your Capability Statement Must Include

- Company name, logo, and contact information.
- Your UEI number and CAGE code.
- Your primary and secondary NAICS codes.
- Your business certifications — WOSB, EDWOSB, small business, etc.
- Core competencies — a concise list of your primary services in plain language.
- Differentiators — what makes your business uniquely qualified.
- Past performance — relevant experience, even if not federal contracts yet.
- Company data — years in business, number of employees, annual revenue range.

Past Performance Does Not Have to Be Federal

If you are new to federal contracting, your past performance section can include commercial clients, government subcontracting work, state or local government contracts, and nonprofit projects. What matters is demonstrating that you have successfully delivered relevant services to paying clients.

Capability Statement Design Tips

- Keep it to one page. Contracting officers review hundreds of these documents.
- Use your brand colors and logo for a professional appearance.
- Use bullet points and short sentences instead of paragraphs.
- Start with your strongest differentiator, the thing that makes you stand out.
- Update it every time you add a new certification, contract, or major client.
- Have a PDF version ready to email and a printed version for in-person meetings.

Building Relationships with Contracting Officers

Federal contracting is not just about submitting bids. The businesses that win again and again are the ones that build relationships with the people who award contracts. Here is how you can start:

Attend Industry Days and Pre-Solicitation Conferences

Many federal agencies host Industry Days, which are public meetings where they share upcoming contracting needs and allow small businesses to introduce themselves. These events are a great way to meet contracting officers in person and learn about opportunities before they are officially posted. Check SAM.gov and agency websites for upcoming events.

Visit Your Local APEX Accelerator

Your local APEX Accelerator (formerly PTAC) offers free one-on-one counseling for government contractors. They can help you identify target agencies, review your capability statement, match you with upcoming bids, and introduce you to local contracting officers. Find your nearest center at aptac-us.org.

Connect With Your Local SBDC

Your Small Business Development Center provides free consulting on all aspects of government contracting, including bid preparation, financial readiness, and growth strategy. Find your nearest center at americassbdc.org.

Attend Small Business Matchmaking Events

The SBA, federal agencies, and prime contractors often host small business matchmaking events. At these events, small business owners can meet with procurement officials and large prime contractors seeking subcontractors. These events are usually free or low-cost and can open doors that a cold email cannot.

Pursue Subcontracting Opportunities

One of the quickest ways to build past performance is by subcontracting with a large prime contractor. Large businesses awarded federal contracts are often required to use small business subcontractors. You can find these opportunities by reaching out to prime contractors, using the SBA SubNet database at web.sba.gov, or networking at matchmaking events.

Your First Contract Does Not Have to Be a Prime Contract
Many successful government contractors started as subcontractors. Subcontracting builds your past performance, familiarizes you with federal contracting requirements, and puts you in the room with prime contractors who may award you larger work over time.

Your First 90 Days Action Plan

Here is a concrete action plan for your first 90 days as a registered federal contractor. Follow this plan, and you will be further ahead than most small businesses that register but never take action.

Timeline	Action Steps
Days 1–10	Create your capability statement. Set up saved searches in SAM.gov for your NAICS codes and set-aside types. Contact your local APEX Accelerator and schedule a free consultation.
Days 11–20	Review 10 to 20 active contract opportunities in your NAICS codes. Study the solicitation language and requirements even if you are not ready to bid. This is research, not commitment.
Days 21–30	Respond to at least one Sources Sought notice. Attend one virtual or in-person industry event. Connect with your local SBDC for a free consultation.

Timeline	Action Steps
Days 31–60	Identify three to five federal agencies whose missions align with your services. Research their small business programs and contracting offices. Begin building your target agency list.
Days 61–90	Submit your first bid or proposal on a contract that genuinely fits your capabilities. Even if you do not win, the experience of writing your first proposal is invaluable preparation for the next one.

The Door Is Open. Walk Through It.

Most small businesses that register on SAM.gov never go after a single contract. They complete the registration, feel a sense of accomplishment, and move on. Months later, the registration expires, and they are back to square one.

You will not be one of those businesses. You have spent time learning the system, understanding your certifications, and building a foundation that most of your competitors never take the time to create.

The federal marketplace is both competitive and huge. There is space for prepared, qualified, and persistent small businesses to succeed. The businesses that win are the ones that show up, stay ready, and keep going even if their first proposal does not work out.

In Chapter 10, we will finish the guide with a complete glossary, key resources, and a roadmap for your next steps. You are almost at the finish line.

Chapter 9 Key Takeaways

- SAM.gov registration is the starting line, not the finish line — active pursuit of opportunities is what leads to contracts.
- Use NAICS codes, set-aside filters, and agency filters together to find the most relevant opportunities.
- Sources Sought notices are your best early opportunity to get in front of contracting officers before formal solicitations are posted.
- Your capability statement is your most important marketing document — create it before you pursue any opportunity.
- Subcontracting is a legitimate and effective path to building past performance for new federal contractors.
- Follow the 90-day action plan — consistent action in your first three months creates momentum that compounds over time.

CHAPTER TEN

Resources, Glossary, and Next Steps: Everything You Need to Keep Moving Forward

You've reached the final chapter. That already sets you apart as a business owner who is truly committed to federal contracting, since most people don't make it this far.

Think of this chapter as your go-to reference. Bookmark it and return whenever you need a quick definition, a contact number, or a reminder about where to find help. All the resources here are free, government-backed, and designed to support small businesses like yours.

We'll finish with your next steps: a clear, practical roadmap for what to do after this guide. You now have valuable knowledge. How you use it is your choice.

Key Federal Resources for Small Business Contractors

All the resources below are free. Use them as your main contacts for help, advice, and opportunities as you move through federal contracting.

Resource	Contact	Best For
SAM.gov	sam.gov	Entity registration, contract opportunities, certification status.

Resource	Contact	Best For
SAM.gov Federal Service Desk	fsd.gov	Registration issues, locked accounts, and technical support.
SBA — Small Business Administration	sba.gov 1-800-827-5722	Business certifications, size standards, loan programs, and the WOSB program.
MySBA Certification Portal	certify.sba.gov	WOSB and EDWOSB certification applications.
APEX Accelerator (formerly PTAC)	aptac-us.org	Free local government contracting counseling and bid matching.
America's SBDC	americassbdc.org	Free small business consulting, financial readiness, and growth strategy.
IRS Business & Specialty Tax Line	irs.gov 1-800-829-4933 Mon–Fri 7 am–7 pm local	EIN verification, business tax questions, and name corrections.
IRS TIN Validation (SAM-specific)	irs.gov 1-866-255-0654	Resolving IRS validation errors specific to SAM.gov registration.
Defense Logistics Agency — CAGE	dla.mil 1-877-352-2255 dlacontactcenter@dla.mil	CAGE code issues and assignments.
Login.gov Help	login.gov/help 1-844-875-6446	Login.gov account issues, locked accounts, and 2FA problems.

Resource	Contact	Best For
Grants.gov	grants.gov 1-800-518-4726	Federal grant opportunities requiring SAM.gov registration.
USASpending.gov	usaspending.gov	Research federal spending, agency budgets, and past contract awards.
SBA SubNet	subcontracting@sba.gov	Find subcontracting opportunities with prime contractors.
SBA Size Standards Tool	sba.gov/size-standards	Verify small business size eligibility by NAICS code.

Additional Resources by State and Region

In addition to national resources, each state has its own network of small-business support groups. Local organizations often know more about regional contracting opportunities and can connect you with state and local government procurement offices as well as federal ones.

- Find your state SBDC network at americassbdc.org/find-your-sbdc.
- Find your local APEX Accelerator at aptac-us.org/find-a-ptac.
- Find SBA district offices at sba.gov/local-assistance.
- Find Women's Business Centers near you at sba.gov/local-assistance/women's-business-centers.
- Find SCORE mentors in your area at score.org.

North Carolina Resources
For readers in North Carolina, your key local resources include the NC Small Business Center Network (ncsbc.net), the NC Military Business Center (ncmbc.us), which specializes in defense contracting, and the NC Department of Administration Office of Historically Underutilized Businesses (HUB) at ncadmin.nc.gov/hub.

Government Contracting Glossary

Federal contracting comes with its own language. This glossary covers the terms you will encounter most frequently as you navigate SAM.gov and pursue federal opportunities. Refer back to this section whenever you encounter an unfamiliar term.

Term	Definition
8(a) Program	An SBA business development program for businesses owned by socially and economically disadvantaged individuals. Certified 8(a) businesses can receive sole-source contracts and compete in set-aside competitions.
APEX Accelerator	Formerly known as Procurement Technical Assistance Centers (PTACs). Government-funded centers that provide free counseling and support to businesses pursuing government contracts at the federal, state, and local levels.
CAGE Code	Commercial and Government Entity code. A five-character identifier assigned by the Defense Logistics Agency to businesses registered in SAM.gov and required for Department of Defense contracts.

Term	Definition
Capability Statement	A one-page marketing document used by small businesses to introduce their services to contracting officers and prime contractors. Includes UEI, CAGE code, NAICS codes, core competencies, and certifications.
Contract Vehicle	A pre-established contracting mechanism that allows federal agencies to purchase goods or services from pre-approved vendors. Examples include GSA Schedules and GWACs.
DFARS	Defense Federal Acquisition Regulation Supplement. Regulations that supplement the FAR specifically for Department of Defense acquisitions.
EFT	Electronic Funds Transfer. The method by which the federal government pays contractors. Requires a valid business bank account on file in SAM.gov.
EIN	Employer Identification Number. A nine-digit number assigned by the IRS to identify a business for tax purposes, required for SAM.gov registration.
EDWOSB	Economically Disadvantaged Woman-Owned Small Business. A federal certification for women-owned businesses that also meet personal financial thresholds for economic disadvantage.
FAR	Federal Acquisition Regulation. The primary set of rules governing federal government purchasing. Contractors must comply with FAR provisions as part of their SAM.gov registration.
GSA Schedule	General Services Administration Multiple Award Schedule. A long-term government-wide contract that allows agencies to purchase commercial products and services at pre-negotiated prices.

Term	Definition
HUBZone	Historically Underutilized Business Zone. A designation for businesses located in and employing residents of economically distressed areas. Certified HUBZone businesses are eligible for set-aside contracts.
Industry Day	A public meeting hosted by a federal agency to present upcoming contracting needs and allow vendors to learn about and respond to future requirements before formal solicitations are released.
NAICS Code	North American Industry Classification System code. A numerical code used to classify businesses by industry and used in SAM.gov to identify your business type and determine small business size eligibility.
Past Performance	A contractor's track record of successfully completing previous contracts. Federal agencies evaluate past performance when selecting contractors. Relevant commercial and government work both count.
Prime Contractor	A business that holds a direct contract with a federal agency. Prime contractors may hire subcontractors to perform portions of the work.
PSC Code	Product and Service Code. A four-character code used to classify the specific products or services being purchased in a federal contract, particularly by the Department of Defense.
Reps and Certs	Representations and Certifications. The legal compliance section of SAM.gov registration, where businesses certify their eligibility and compliance with federal acquisition regulations.
SAM.gov	System for Award Management. The official U.S. government website where businesses register to do business with the federal government, manage their entity information, and search for contract opportunities.

Term	Definition
SBA	Small Business Administration. The federal agency responsible for supporting small businesses through loans, certifications, contracting programs, and advocacy.
SBDC	Small Business Development Center. Publicly funded centers hosted by universities and colleges that provide free consulting and low-cost training to small business owners.
Set-Aside Contract	A federal contract reserved for competition among businesses with specific designations such as small business, WOSB, EDWOSB, veteran-owned, or HUBZone.
Sole Source Contract	A contract awarded to a single vendor without competitive bidding. Allowed under specific circumstances, including 8(a) program participation and certain emergencies.
Sources Sought Notice	A market research posting on SAM.gov where a federal agency gauges whether qualified businesses exist for a potential future requirement. Responding does not commit you to bidding.
Subcontractor	A business hired by a prime contractor to perform a portion of a federal contract. Subcontracting is a common path for new government contractors to build experience and past performance.
UEI	Unique Entity Identifier. A 12-character alphanumeric code assigned by SAM.gov to every registered entity, replacing the DUNS number in April 2022 as the official federal business identifier.
WOSB	Woman-Owned Small Business. A federal certification for businesses at least 51% owned and controlled by one or more women who are U.S. citizens. Eligible for set-aside contracts in designated industries.

Your Next Steps Roadmap

You've completed the guide. Here's a step-by-step roadmap showing what to do right away, in the next 30 days, and over the next 90 days.

This Week

- Complete your SAM.gov registration if you have not already done so.
- Set your annual renewal reminder in your calendar for 60 days before your expiration date.
- Create your capability statement using the guidance in Chapter 9.
- Set up at least two saved searches in SAM.gov for your NAICS codes and set-aside types.
- Apply for WOSB or EDWOSB certification at certify.sba.gov if you are eligible.

This Month

- Contact your local APEX Accelerator for a free consultation.
- Contact your local SBDC for a free business assessment.
- Review 20 or more contract opportunities in your NAICS code to understand the market.
- Respond to at least one Sources Sought notice.
- Attend one industry day, matchmaking event, or small business networking event.

Next 90 Days

- Submit your first bid or proposal on a contract that genuinely fits your capabilities.
- Identify three to five target agencies and research their small business programs.
- Explore subcontracting opportunities by contacting subcontracting@sba.gov and reaching out to prime contractor websites directly.
- Build a government contracting network through LinkedIn, local events, and agency outreach.
- Review and update your SAM.gov registration to ensure all information is up to date.

You Are Not Alone on This Journey

The federal contracting community is more accessible than it looks from the outside. There are free resources, supportive organizations, and fellow small business owners who have walked this path before you. Reach out, ask questions, and keep moving forward. The opportunities are real. The support is available. All that is left is for you to claim it.

A Final Word

When you first saw SAM.gov, it probably felt overwhelming. The screens were crowded, the terms were new, and the process seemed made for someone with more experience than you had at the time.

But you kept moving forward. You gathered your documents, set up your Login.gov account, completed the registration steps, learned about your UEI, understood your certifications, and built a foundation that most small business owners never take the time to build.

That's a big achievement. It's what sets apart businesses that only dream about federal contracting from those that actually succeed.

The federal marketplace needs what you offer. Agencies have real needs, real budgets, and real commitments to working with small businesses, especially those owned by women. Your place at the table isn't given; it's earned. And you've earned it.

Now, go win those contracts!

Quick Reference: Most Important Contacts

- SAM.gov Federal Service Desk: fsd.gov | Mon–Fri 8 am–8 pm EST
- IRS Business & Specialty Tax Line: 1-800-829-4933 | Mon–Fri 7 am–7 pm local time
- IRS TIN Validation (SAM-specific): 1-866-255-0654
- DLA CAGE Help Desk: 1-877-352-2255 | dlacontactcenter@dla.mil
- Login.gov Help: login.gov/help | 1-844-875-6446
- SBA: sba.gov | 1-800-827-5722
- MySBA Certification Portal (WOSB/EDWOSB): certify.sba.gov
- APEX Accelerator (formerly PTAC): aptac-us.org
- America's SBDC: americassbdc.org

www.ingramcontent.com/pod-product-compliance
Lightning Source LLC
LaVergne TN
LVHW022014200926
848481LV00007B/2390
9798995877608